Testimonies Of The Spirit

Philip Broussard

Presentation by *BookLeaf Publishing*

Web: www.bookleafpub.com

E-mail: info@bookleafpub.com

ISBN: 9789358314960

First edition 2023

Soldier of God

In a world taken over by evil,
God chooses carefully his people.
A young man with troubles he can barely
withstand,
Calls out to God and asks for His plan.
He gives God all his struggle and all his pain.
In return, eternal life he would gain.
Now the young man is ready to move forward.
God equips him with a Bible as his sword.
The young man is ready to fight,
And this time his team is right.
Battle after battle the devil cannot win.
For once in his life, the young man is free of sin.
Full of frustration satan increases the temptation.
But now the soldier of God's army is the size of
a nation.
Finally the enemy realizes it has no chance.
The soldier of God sings victory in Jesus with
his victory dance.

True Love

There is nothing better than the feeling you get when you truly love someone. Like no matter what she has done, will do, or has been through will ever change the fact that you will always have her back. Through all the ups and downs, smiles, and frowns, you will never leave her side, but always be around. Ready to answer when she calls, be there to catch her when she falls. Always there to wipe her tears away and put a smile on her face. Remember that love is a marathon. It's not a sprint. Love's not that kind of race. It takes understanding, patience, and sacrifice. For love you must be willing to pay the ultimate price. Like no matter what, day or night, wrong or right, you will always be there to keep her safe and hold her tight. Be there to help protect her from the dark and keep her in the light. Give her God's heart from the start and never take it back. How can you not love a feeling like that?

A Beautiful Gift from God

I truly am humbled at the level of your
greatness. It seemed at times I would never
receive this blessing but prevailed with patience.
Filled with joy when my journey with You led
me to her.
She was so beautiful and sweet.
I thought my life was complete.
I found my one true love sent from You up
above and nothing could be better.
Only I let my guard down by forgetting that the
devil is clever.
It's easy to lose sight of Your grand scheme by
shifting focus to the craziness that this world can
bring.
So now this beautiful gift that I acquired, the one
true thing my heart most desired, was foolishly
accepted because I neglected to think about all
that it required.
A blessing can become a lesson quick when a
woman and not God is your first pick.
Lord I just wanted to accept this gift that you
have gracefully given but then seemed to forget
that it's because of You that I am still living.
So, to my knees I fall and my hands I raise as I
give You all the glory and all the praise.

Your will is still my will, Your plan is still my
plan, and this beautiful gift I will always cherish
but now I truly understand, that the only way of
ever having this gift again,
is by returning it into Your mighty hand.

Be Real Stay True

I've come a long way but still I have so far to go. I got so much love to give and for Jesus I want to live but sometimes it's hard to show. Pain, I know all too well, but I know it prepares me for the testimony I'll tell and if it reaches one person well, then it was all worth it. Good Lord, my salvation, I know I don't deserve it on account of all my mistakes, but You sent Your only Son to die for me and He was perfect. So, I live under grace, and I thank you for that because when I sit back and think of where I could have been, then I'm suddenly grateful for where I'm at. There's no telling what the next man goes through so it could always be worse, and I truly believe the possibilities are endless as long as I put You first. It's that simple but sometimes it's hard to understand so that's why I put my trust in You Lord because I know I'm just a man. I fall short daily, but I continue to grow as long as I keep pushing forward and stay focused on You, one day it will show. My struggle is for a bigger purpose and at times I feel I don't deserve this but then I humble myself, get on my knees and pray. Ask for Your strength just to get through the day because I know it all works together for my good and You will make a way. You always do and I know that Your love is true so that's why when times get hard and I don't know where to go or what to do, I call on You. You haven't let me down yet and You never will. That's why every day I strive to be like You and that's what it means to be real. That's what it means to stay true. Live for Jesus and do what He would do. It won't be easy and some battles you'll lose but stay true to who you are. Don't lose yourself when times get hard. You will make some mistakes but understand you're already forgiven. So, make your next move your best move, accept Jesus into your heart and forever you will be living.

My Deliverance

They say faith it, don't fake it and life isn't fair but it is what you make it. I said that a long time ago, in the same dorm where rules were violated, and moral codes annihilated while others participated in games where they'd yell domino. You can't tell me God isn't real. Just on the mere fact that when I look back at where He brought me from. Not to mention the evil intention that led to divine intervention when I thought my life was done. I met Christ the Son. You see death I was near it, so I gave out my last cries but then I was baptized in the Holy Spirit. It was something that words could never explain, nor could they ever obtain the fullness of the goodness that I would taste. I saw evil face to face but then it disappeared without a trace when Jesus and His angels entered the place. Talk about a change of pace and what a waste I could have been and should have been if it hadn't been for His grace. But it takes what it takes and even though deep within there was a desire to go higher I was still knee deep in sin. It only led to some lonely nights with holy fights and on some of them I'll never speak again. Have you ever experienced angels and demons playing tug of war for your soul? I was on my dad's couch and my last route was to reach for the remote control as I turned on the bible movie while waiting to see what would happen to me. Another close call where I almost lost it all on my path to surrender. It happened in 2017 next to a hall that was green in the month of December. I hit my knees giving it all to the One who frees, and I vividly remember waking up that night with one last fight, but it was no contender. The demon of addiction that caused so much affliction was mad that it had to go. It was time to answer my calling as I took it all in watching it drift away far from my soul. I was delivered. Thank You Jesus.

"But by God's grace I am what I am, and His grace toward me was not ineffective. However, I worked more than any of them, yet not I, but God's grace that was with me."

1 Corinthians 15:10 HCSB

Dear Holy Spirit

You've been with me since the start of it, never left my side through any part of it. You've been the heart of it, my will to keep me going. You filled me with this knowing, then kept me safe and secure when my heart was far from pure. It's undeniable how reliable You are. You were there with me every time I put the poison in my vein, and all the times I chose to sulk in my pain. My body was supposed to be a temple for You to dwell in, but instead I chose to be sinful and let hell in. I was selfish and rebellious, yet You loved me still, patiently waiting for the right time to remind me of what was real. I constantly pushed You away, but no matter how far I would stray, You were there to stay. I tried to hide in the dark, and every time I thought all hope was lost, You provided the spark to keep me going. I remember I was glowing the first night I met You. Then it seems like the very next day I acted in the same sinful way, how easily I would forget You. What about the time You told me to flush the needle with all that evil in it? I hesitated for a minute but was grateful when I did it. It was only then when I chose to listen that You filled me with Your presence to let me know what I was missing with another reminder. I was at that house on the couch sitting next to the recliner. That moment was just a component of who You are. With You it was always divine, and even though You were last on my mind, You were always right on time. How could You love someone like me when I disobeyed You nightly? And despite me, You and the angels would remove all dangers when the darkness would come to fight me. That's real love. But when daylight came, I hid in shame like I didn't know Your name. That's real pain. I did my best not to enter your rest. I was the definition of self-destruction, but even then, my intuition was Your instruction, because when I willingly chose my own path to take, You still let me know where not to go, and if I was headed for a big mistake. I thank You for that, and now that I look back, I have much to repent for. From the moment You would enter all the way up until my surrender, I rejected all that You were sent for, but since then it's only meant more. Now I have this hunger and thirst to keep You first and never give in with an inward desire sparked from a flame of fire to let the living waters burst forth from within. So, Holy Spirit forgive me, and thank You for always being with me. I decrease for a full release. Have Your way and fill me

with Your peace. Thy will be done in Jesus'
mighty name. Amen.

Who Would Have Thought?

I mean really, who would have thought? The devil set the trap and that was a wrap but praise God I was blood bought. I was all but on that train headed towards eternal suffering and pain but then He called my name. I wanted to answer but didn't know what to say. I withstood all that I could stand for then the Holy Spirit came into pray. If you knew me then you knew I didn't have much of a chance. Not with the jail sentence, hospital visits, and all my crazy rants. My brother Jody didn't. He said, "Brouss it's a miracle today to see you living," and he wasn't kidding. My brother Shane said he never stopped praying for me, and when I went to prison my big brother Josh was waiting for me. He was hoping and praying that we would finally get along. Now we get along, he's been with me all along. Only God could write such a wrong into a beautiful song. You see, our ticket has already been paid for. The moment Jesus rose from the grave the road was paved for us to walk into all that we were made for. Praise the Lord. His way is way more than we could fully grasp or ask, and His grace is not an excuse to sin but an opportunity to bring forth truth from

within. So, I pray that you give up control and
let the Holy Spirit guide your soul into all things
that only heaven brings. Where all rejoice and
every angel sings from a wonderful essence with
a powerful presence of divine beauty. From
yours truly, one of those He chose to pay the
price for. A soldier in Christ Lord. In Jesus'
mighty name. Amen.

They say to live is to suffer and to love is to hurt. Well I wonder if that's what Jesus was thinking as He hung from the 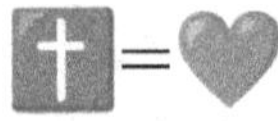 and His blood hit the dirt. It was all for love but I can only imagine the pain He felt. That's why His love is truly powerful and the most hardened hearts it surely can melt. You see I could know it all and show it all but without love I would gain nothing. It's only when I get out self and love for the sake of something else then do I truly gain something. Love keeps no record of wrongs, so to hold a grudge why even try, and it's no love lost because the love I now give comes from the main supply. If I try to love from self then it just won't last and it ain't real, because agape love is not based off the emotions I feel. It's about putting aside all my lust and all my pride. Loving with truth and letting the Holy Spirit be the guide. Feelings are cunning, they can get your heart racing and blood pumping. But love is patient and love is kind. It endures all by showing support and giving them time. You never know what's on another person's mind. It's about seeking to understand before being understood. Love is about sacrifice and being willing to suffer for a greater good. It's about loving for nothing in return because I can't expect others to know what I've learned nor expect them to give the same grace or love at the same pace. All I can control is how I love for when I meet Jesus face to face. So the aim will always be the same, and that is to glorify the Father in Jesus name. He's calling me out to deeper water but I can never grow if I don't let go of the resentments and dissapointments that I harbor. Jesus had no regrets when He went to the ✝ because with that type of love there was so much to gain that He couldn't count it as a loss. So from Your willingness of the sacrifice to the power of Your resurrection, Lord I give You my life, complete me in Your love and give me direction. Thy will be done in Jesus name, amen.

To Whom the Spirit Pleases: True Surrender

If a wise heart is called discerning and pleasant speech increases learning (Prov 16:21), then Lord give me the insight to make my steps right while every bridge that leads back to my past stays forever burning. I live in the now and no longer will I attempt to control the how. I can honestly say that I trust this journey. Other than looking back to learn from, my past does not concern me. I no longer trip or stress over what's to come because the Father's will is perfect, so I stay focused on His Son. Thy will be done. I say this with security, Jesus is the only cure for me. So, Holy Spirit work through all my insecurities and remove the impurities as I gain spiritual maturity. I know the battle that's in store for me so it's the Spirit that goes to war for me. Thank you, Jesus. It was His blood that was spilled and now this vessel is special because it's Holy Spirit filled. Truth is revealed. I'm blood washed and made new in His righteousness so there's no reason for me to be fighting this. My heart takes delight in this. I level up and grow as I learn to let go with another surrender. I find out that when I remove myself, the devil is no contender.

He's only a pretender that operates in lies and fear, and all that false evidence he can try and supply, but it no longer appears real. I have the mind of Christ (1 Cor 2:16) and God removed the veil. Praise God. He gives us this treasure in a clay jar (2 Cor 4:7), so even in the darkest of nights and hardest of fights, you can still see His light from afar. That's hope. So, Lord plant the seed that grows a tree of life to produce fruit that's ripe so that the multitudes can feed. This is for the ones in need. Blessed are those who are poor in spirit (Matt 5:3). I know life is hard but don't jump out that car, give Jesus the wheel and let Him steer it. It's a fight and this world can lead you left when you thought it was right but have hope in the unseen (2 Cor 4:18) and pray for endurance. Then go read Romans 8:18 and thank Him for that blessed assurance. It always gets greater later when we put our life in the hands of the Creator. The Maker of the heavens and earth, the stars and sun. In the mighty name of Jesus, thy will be done. Amen.

To whom the Spirit Pleases: A Blessed Life

The Lord is gracious to those who are afflicted and alone. I know this to be true because His Spirit came through when I was lost and on my own. He considered my afflictions, conflictions, and all my trouble. Then It was Psalm 34:7 and His holy angels came from heaven on the double. Thank You Father. He removed the veil and showed me what was real when He gave me sight. I saw the light and only good things come from above so swallow your pride and walk in love because it's a spiritual fight. It's by Spirit, not by might and I'm forever grateful for that faithful night. I was forever changed, and to the natural it might seem strange but even before my birth the meeting was prearranged. I thought I had no worth, but heaven came down to earth and met in my heart for a beautiful exchange. Praise God. It could never be fully explained but salvation was truly obtained. Now my heart is set apart from the world, but that doesn't mean I no longer have a heart for the world. It's just now I've been commissioned with a mission to shine His light to reach all that is dark in the world. Soldier for

Christ. It's on Him that I cast all my cares because there is nothing else that compares to what He has in store, so I endure for the joy that lay before. It will only be greater and more than I could ever imagine or fathom and nothing is random. He works everything together for the good so don't grow weary in doing what Jesus would. For the ground that endures the heavy rain will produce the vegetation that will be the inspiration for others to do the same. Every miracle that occurs in the spiritual isn't always made visible in the physical. So, keep planting seeds and doing good deeds because it's usually the one that you think is not watching is actually the one that sees. Encourage your sisters and brothers and pray for others such as your enemies and those that persecute. Remember, God can use anyone, we all have a work to do. So, love more, judge less, and no matter the cost pick up your ✝ and live the life that's best. A life where you never have to hurry, worry, or stress. A life that's blessed. In Jesus name, thy will be done, amen.

To Whom the Spirit Pleases: Jesus is There

If one person gives freely only to gain more (Proverbs 11:24) then Lord for Your love and Your light let this vessel be an open door to provide healing for the spiritually sick and poor. Let the wind of Your Spirit blow through the windows of my soul and fan the the flame that will spark the light in others to do the same. In Jesus name. Fill this heart with compassion and courage that overflows to the mouth to speak life with truth in love to edify and encourage. Lord let this mind be mindful of who You are and how You operate because to look after orphans and widows in their distress is the only religion that I'll indoctrinate (James 1:27). Holy Spirit have Your way. A life of service in Christ's purpose is my only pleasure and the mystery of this adventure will reveal the hidden treasure (Colossians 2:2-3). A beautiful gift and a great reward is what I desire to acquire as I delight in the Lord while moving forward (Psalm 37:4). I press on. The old me is non-existent and even though the enemy is persistent God's grace is sufficient (2 Corinthians 12:9). I'm grateful. His love is where it begins and when it's shared it

comes together forever because it never ends (1
Corinthians 13:8). But His love is not typical
because it doesn't have to be reciprocal for it to
be effective. It will go where it's directed and
just know Jesus is there if you ever feel
neglected or rejected. He was disrespected, spit
on, and hit on, but no one could ever truly say
that there was anything He ever did wrong. They
tried and in the garden was where out to the
Father He cried (Luke 22:44) before He went to
the cross and died after they falsely accused and
lied. Through it all with joy He endured
(Hebrews 12:2) and victory over death (1
Corinthians 15:54-57) was forever secured. King
Jesus. He gave His life so we could live on but
not live on in sin because underneath the flesh is
a Spirit that's deep within yearning to change the
heart's image of all women and men. So, take
heart but don't grieve, just believe and let Him
in. Life is a journey home that leads up above
(Proverbs 15:24) and transformation is a
process. So, I pray that through His love you're
an object in motion with grace in progress. Now
to Him who is able to do above and beyond all
that we could think or ask (Ephesians 3:20), the
One for who there is no such thing as too big of
a task (Psalm 111:2), redeem and restore you
from the troubles of your past, and sanctify you
completely (1 Thessalonians 5:23) into a new

creation (2 Corinthians 5:17) that ever lasts.
Father through Your Son may Your perfect will
be done. Holy Spirit have Your way in Jesus
name I pray. Amen.

So I Write

Don't really have the words to write, but still I write. And it can be hard to speak words when I tend to stumble and fumble with syllables and verbs, so I write. But I can't do it on my own. And these words could never come from me alone. So, Lord help me write. Fuel the desire and spark the fire that will provide the light to what I write. Flood this mind with all that is divine so whether day or night, dark or bright, still I write. Lord speak in me from deep within me as Your Spirit takes flight in what I write. Holy Spirit have Your way. Be the inspiration and insulation of the words that flow from this broken and dishonest hand. Let them be the warmth and the substance to help draw those You chose into Your promised land. What is man that You're mindful of him? I mean every component with every moment and Your perfect timing of them. Selah. Every detail of my heart was on retail from the start. But even then, Your Spirit would not depart. I don't get it. I mean it's not logical, but then again neither was the Father's love for the son that went prodigal. God sits on the throne, and He stands alone. Yet somehow, He chose to call this heart His home. I can't explain it. My only hope to obtain it more while my mind stays in heaven with my feet planted on the floor as I anticipate and wait for what's in store. His thoughts are much higher, and His will is perfect, and you'll see it transpire but it's best if you search it. True self-discovery is a luxury, and it didn't start until I had enough of me. I found myself grounded in a world that I wasn't founded in which means I'm not of it, but I've been tasked by the Lord to be an ambassador which means I place nothing above it. I have a kingdom to represent with purpose that's heaven sent, and I pray His message is sent to every earthly resident until it becomes evident. So, Lord let Your kingdom come and Your will be done on earth as is it in heaven with total restoration just as it was on day seven. And as for me Lord, slice and dice every part of this heart with Your double edge sword. Break me down and make me sound until all that I am is the Lion and the Lamb as I continue to fight the good fight with these words that I write. In Jesus mighty name. Amen.

God's Heartbeat, Gift of Love, and Spirit of Truth

God's heartbeat is an echo of His love that comes from above with a vibration from a sensation that guides to you to what is true, and the Holy Spirit confirms it through visions, dreams, and other really cool things. What it brings, is a piece of heaven to earth and a glimpse of what's about to give birth. We serve a perfect God. His love is vast, and it ever lasts. Not only does it right the wrongs but it forgives the past. It breaks down but it builds up, and it empties but it also fills up. It takes what's meant for evil and turns it to good, and it makes known what could never be understood. A gift is a gift, and it's not for us to resist and question it, just rest in it. It's expressed in many different forms, and it breaks through all cultural norms with a full measure to bind His people together forever. No curse or dam could ever stop the river of love that flows from the blood of the Lamb. Praise God. It's also experienced through different types of blessings, such as toughness with discipline and life lessons, but also through softness with warmth and tenderness, but both with pure genuineness. There's brotherly love, fatherly love, and motherly love also known as the cover me love, because sometimes His love has to smother us and cover us from anything that could harm us or trouble us. Then there's the missing rib love. The most intense of them all. A love too deep to make sense of it all. The human mind could never fully comprehend a love this divine, so He sends His Spirit to bind with ours, in order to link the spiritual to the physical, just as He did with the moon and the stars. He speaks, and we listen when our soul is broken, and our heart is open. For us to see, we have to be, and what an impossible feat His love will complete when we step in faith and get out of our comfort seat. So, Lord continue to break this soul until it fits the mold, and let Your heartbeat send a jumpstart to my feet to step in Your will with the Holy Spirit confirming what's real, as He walks by my side in stride helping me along the way, resting in Your love all throughout the day. In Jesus mighty name I pray. Amen.

To My Missing Rib

I can see you. You are beautiful, gentle, and caring. I'm not concerned with your outward appearance as far how you look, or what you're wearing. I'm drawn to your heart. It shines a light that reflects to His face. Our meeting place. From your heart to mine, it's only through His that we align to form something divine. One heartbeat where three hearts meet. God's love. The perfect bond of unity. Him, you, and me. One in three and three in one. Just like the Father, Holy Spirit, and Son. Completion.

Psalms 37:4

I may get lonely but I'm never alone. And ever since 2013 when the Holy Spirit stepped on the scene this truth has been known. Jesus said it was better that He went away so that the Helper would come. So that He could walk beside us to lead us and guide us back to where we are from. So, if I'm not alone then why do I still get lonely? Why is it time after time I find myself in a place of if only? If only I had someone to go to church with and flirt with. To love and hurt with. Live life to the fullest every day all the way back to the dirt with. Then maybe things would be better right? Or is it wrong to think it would be better to have someone with to journey along? Cause truth be told at the beginning in the time of old the enemy led us to believe that we were lacking something. Had us reaching to the tree for a snack but the fact is we were lacking nothing. We were already filled with a full course meal. In His presence with eternal pleasures is where it's real. But even then, it was woman with man, and what it sounds like to me is the two as a pair together in the garden to share forever was God's original plan. But I know for everything there is a place with a time,

and you can't make haste of what's divine.
There's a rhyme and a reason for every season.
And the season I'm in is not to grieve for a
friend, a partner, and wife til the end, but to
leave it with Him. So, Holy Spirit before I reach
for it again, take this cycle off spin. Remind me
of the life of a friend who endured with His life
to the end to make us right from our sin. I'm
delighting in Him.

Love Has A Name

Her beauty is no longer in my sight but still I write, and the warmth of the love in her hug is no longer within an arms grasp but this too shall pass, and the light in her eyes no longer leaves my heart in demise, but still I rise. Her hands no longer gently caress and press against my shoulders when I pray anymore but still my knees hit the floor. What is it for, this life? Well, if it's for love then love is better than life itself. And what is wealth? The currency of love. Something without measure, an endless treasure filled with intangible pleasure. Something from what the eyes can't see, and the hands can't touch, something that sets us free and doesn't cost that much. Just us, and faith and trust. So, what is love? And if it's better than life then who gave their life for love? Do you know Him? A Bridegroom who faced doom to bring back His bride to the garden a beautiful place to reside? A Husband's sacrifice that raised His wife back to life in love? Well, if that's the case then count me in, because love is a place that I found me in. But let me explain this love has a name. And even though two hearts could never be the same, they're both found in the same place positioned with the same face full of mercy and grace. And this Name holds weight. It's been known to separate those who live off of feelings and those who are willing to wait. And let me just say that God is great. He sent His only Son, the only One who could display this kind of love. And so, we hope in this blessed assurance with endurance through sufferings as He ushers in all that we trust Him in. And as we get close to the end, let me boast in the friend who sticks closer than a brother, the one true lover who never displayed anything other than that one true love in which He sees us. His name is Jesus. Amen.

Do Not Fear

DO NOT FEAR, if you can look to the clouds see where the storm is, then you can look to the crowds and see how crazy the norm is. The time is near, and He says to be the light of the world, so the shine is here. My mind is clear, and it's only been a little more than four revealing years with an outpour of healing tears since Jesus took the wheel to steer. He understands. His pierced hands and blood stains are the reason for no more dope in my veins. Now a life of struggle and pain no longer remains. Glory to God. The thought of it all may seem odd. That even though I could never be tough or worthy enough it was predestined before my birth that He would remove me and use me to bring heaven to earth. Thy kingdom come. To some it may seem dumb or sound downright crazy that I would no longer be conformed but transformed into the image of the One who made me. But to the spiritual it's truth with the knowing being proof. A city on a hill glowing through the roof and beaming out the window screaming all are welcome in, but you can't bring your sin though. There's grace for that. So, take up your mat when you hear the call. Then follow Him though it all and He will

lead you to where the place is at. The Good
Shepherd. And I can't escape the fact that every
day it becomes more practical to make my steps
more tactical with the Holy Spirit being the
admiral leading to the ones considered collateral.
It's a war out there and this world doesn't fight
fair. And what we're really looking for is neither
here nor there. Christ paid the price then planted
a seed from which the multitudes could feed,
and the birds of the air could make their nest and
find their rest. Just look beneath the skin deep
within and you'll see that we're truly blessed. So
Heavenly Father let Your kingdom root down
deep into my soul and let it grow until it's all
that I know and all that I show with the Holy
Spirit in control. Let the eyes behold what's
already been told and watch it unfold. Father,
there are many who have been led astray with
the ways of this world leaving them in dismay. I
pray that they break away and head this way.
Holy Spirit give us the ears to hear and the
words to say as Your kingdom delegates to the
minds left reprobate. To put some truth to it, You
the only One who can do it. So let our praises
elevate and all of heaven celebrate while the
hurts of the past depart from their heart as they
rest at Your feet to a victory that's sweet
knowing that they've chosen the good part. In
Jesus mighty name, amen.

Do You Hope For More?

Do you hope for more?
Are you spiritually broke and poor, bruised and
sore?
Won a few battles but feel like you're losing the
war?
Then this message is for you, and don't be
alarmed or result to self-harm the testing reveals
what is true.
He's making us new.
Just so you know there's a furnace with your
name on it but when you come out, you'll be
clothed in a robe that's white shining bright
without a stain on it.
And you won't be in it alone.
The King of heaven and earth who ever since
birth has been knocking at the door to make your
heart His throne.
If you open up and receive then you will achieve
more than you could ever imagine or fathom.
All you have to do is believe.
And this isn't a time to grieve on what could
have been or should have been.
Stick to the One who sticks closer than a friend.

Those who endure to the end shall be saved, and
before time began, He fulfilled your days which
means the road has already been paved.
It's said and done.
Remember, He bled and won, now we get to
walk and talk with our Father through the Son.
And when the weight gets too heavy, lean on the
Rock whose balance is always steady.
For every situation that was dire, every
tribulation that would transpire, and every valley
that brought me lower was another opportunity
for Him to take me higher.
My Lord, I'm forevermore in the pleasure of the
treasure I found in You.
I'm bound to You.
Though all the highs and lows my soul goes up
and down on solid ground with You.
When we're seated above with You, we see a
lovely view.
Redemption and restoration with all things new
from ascension to a destination where my spirit
man sings to You.
My soul clings to You.
Lord apart from You I'm filthy and reckless
eating sin for breakfast.
But to hear the words "job well done" from my
Messiah is only thing I desire to have marked off
my checklist.

So do for me Lord what I most certainly could
never do for me.
Love me perfectly and stay true to me because
You do it beautifully.
Honestly, it's only Your sovereignty that keeps
me in Your will.
I get to moving too fast trying to improve from
the past and start to reach for the wheel.
Teach me how to pause for the cause and be still.
Continue to make me new as You take me to
what's true until it becomes real.
Holy Spirit have Your way, in Jesus mighty
name I pray.
Amen.

A Beautiful Gift From God II

It's better to love than not love at all, and Lord how could I ever doubt Your route when You're the One who's above it all. Feelings come and they go. Sometimes they're high and other times they're low, but one thing that remains through the joy and the pains is Your love and beautiful gift from above. I believe it, and now that my spiritual eyes perceive it, it's on me to receive it. Into my heart and into my mind I receive what's true and follow through with this love that's divine. It's good because You're good, and You make it known with Your glory to be shown when it can't be understood. I call, and You answer with great and incomprehensible things that only heaven brings. Let every angel sing and all of heaven rejoice because you gave your child the choice and he chose love. He's been broken down and opened up unto the point that he thought all hope was up. It was so that the Lord could fill this cup that it may never pass but overflow and ever last from His hand. I've entered the greener grass of the land, the other side, one of the reasons my brother died. Now he lives to see his little brother be all that he was created to be, the husband and father that God has made him to be. But it's not for me, it's for we. It's for us, so Lord into Your hands I put my trust and give You my life, as You fill me with this love and beautiful gift from above, my wife. In Jesus mighty name. Amen.

Dear Holy Spirit II

You put this gleam in me. Make things clean in me. Still don't understand what You had seen in me. I'm just glad You're changing the scenery. These words could never fully explain or truly contain what You mean to me. That's no lie, but for the sake of my gratitude let me try. My attitude and behavior were far from the reflection of my Lord and Savior. Couldn't love myself much less love my neighbor. I returned to my vomit more times than I'd like to remember, but with everyone You nudged me closer towards another surrender. You didn't condone it, so I owned it. Didn't have the strength for it but the grace You loaned it. The nights when I was lonely, it was You and me only with the tears that I shed kneeling next to my bed. Or what about the dream where I felt Your touch when my grandma rubbed my head? She used to do that back in the day when I was a child before I ran wild and lost my way. I thank You for the restoration, and to all the things You're making new there is no estimation. So, I won't even try. I just pray You build the endurance for me to reach the destination with You on high. Through trial and error, rejection and correction, You

allowed me to live and give, but kept me in Your
protection. And I thank You for that. You taught
me how to guard my heart, and comforted me
through the pain that came from learning how to
master that art. Now I'm ready for a new start.
But everything that scares me is what You
prepare me for, and the only thing that I ask is
that You prepare me more. Don't let me step into
if I'm not ready. If the time ain't right and this
heart's not steady. Cause truth be told it takes
being bold and the weight of Your glory can
seem so heavy. But when the pressure comes
just press more oil. Keep me planted down in the
ground with the good soil next to the river so the
fruit won't spoil. What I'm saying or praying for
is to stay in Your Open Door with the wisdom
and vision to continue to move in my Holy Spirit
groove only towards what You approve. Holy
Spirit have Your way. In Jesus mighty name I
pray. Amen.

Do We Remain Silent?

Do we remain silent? The atmosphere is violent, overruled by a giant tyrant but nobody seems to notice. As more and more distractions shift our focus from the elephant that grows bigger in the room. Impending doom and a King coming soon. And what do we do? Follow celebrities who celebrate and delegate for a different kingdom that brings them money, fame, and power that won't amount to a thing in the last hour. Then where will we be? Go to the scriptures in the book and take a look to see. Where your treasure is there your heart is and where your pleasure is that's where your start is. I pray it's in the right place. Mercy and grace are for the ones with the blood on their door for when the time comes of His wrath to pour. And just take a look at the world all around with everything burning to the ground. It's already begun but the good news is that it's already been won. But if you don't know that victory or have this liberty then you will just be left with only the misery. There's only one name and one King who will reign. He's the one to fear but hold dear cause He wipes every tear and heals every pain. Do you know Him? And if you do, will

you show them? The time is now to reach for the
plow. For the harvest is ripe, not the time to
argue or gripe about which doctrine is right.
Won't they know us by how we love each other?
And it's an intense love for one another that will
cover a multitude of sins leading up to the day
when it all ends. So why don't we come together
to show that being a part of the body of Christ is
far better than anything anyone could ever argue
about before time runs out? Lord for the sake of
Your name let your servants not go without. Let
Your kingdom come, and Your will be done as
You bring the rain to put an end to this drought.
Holy Spirit have Your way, in Jesus mighty
name I pray. Amen.